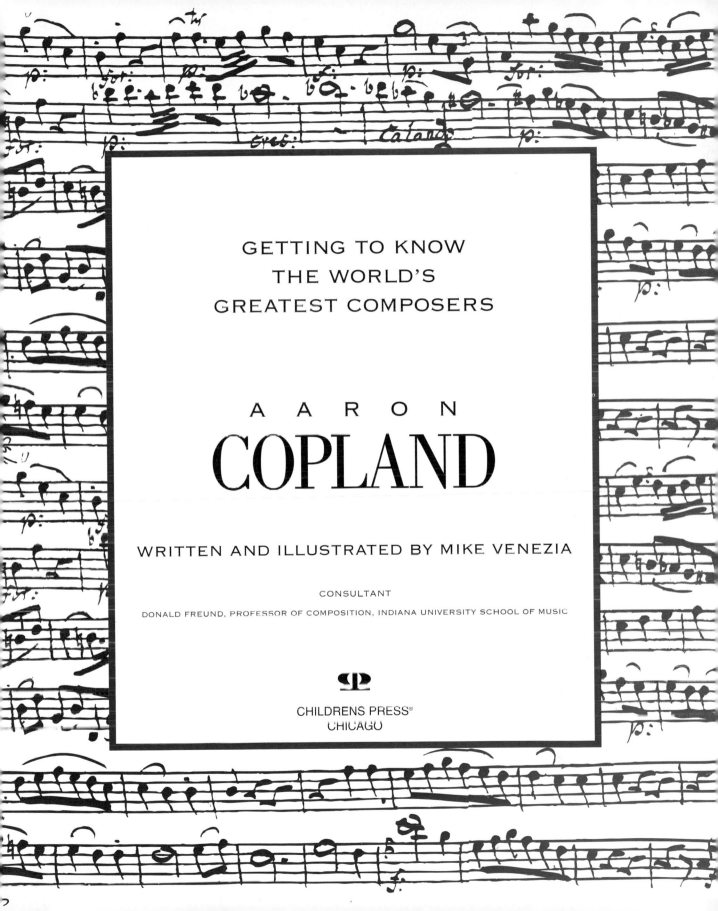

GETTING TO KNOW THE WORLD'S GREATEST COMPOSERS

A A R O N

COPLAND

WRITTEN AND ILLUSTRATED BY MIKE VENEZIA

CONSULTANT

DONALD FREUND, PROFESSOR OF COMPOSITION, INDIANA UNIVERSITY SCHOOL OF MUSIC

CHILDRENS PRESS®
CHICAGO

For my parents, Eugene and Patricia Venezia

Picture Acknowledgments
Music on the cover, Stock Montage, Inc.; 3, AP/Wide World Photos; 10, Library of Congress;
13 (top), Yale University Art Gallery, Bequest of Dorothea Dreier to the Collection Société Anonyme;
13 (bottom), Purchased with funds from the Coffin Fine Arts Trust, Nathan Emory Coffin Collection of
the Des Moines Art Center, 1962.21; 14, 15 (left), Stock Montage, Inc; 15 (right), AP/Wide World Photos;
16, UPI/Bettmann; 17, Musée des Arts Décoratifs, Paris, photograph © L. Sully-Jaulmes;
18-19, Archibald John Motley, Jr., American, 1891-1981, *Blues*, oil on canvas, 1929, 80 x 100.3 cm,
Lent by Archie Motley and Valerie Gerrard Browne, 41.1988, photograph © 1994 The Art Institute of
Chicago, All Rights Reserved; 20, Stock Montage, Inc.; 24, Los Angeles County Museum of Art,
Gift of Mr. and Mrs. Milton W. Lipper, from the Milton W. Lipper Estate; 26, The Bettmann Archive; 27,
Martha Swope/Dance Theatre of Harlem; 29, The Saint Louis Art Museum Purchase; 30 (top)
Stephen R. Dolan/American Ballet Theatre; 30 (bottom), Martha Swope/Martha Graham Dance Company;
31 (top), Culver Pictures, Inc.; 31 (bottom), AP/Wide World Photos; 32, Stock Montage, Inc.

Project Editor: Shari Joffe
Design: PCI Design Group, San Antonio, Texas
Photo Research: Jan Izzo

Library of Congress Cataloging–in–Publication Data

Venezia, Mike.
    Aaron Copland / written and illustrated by Mike Venezia.
    p.   cm. -- (Getting to know the world's greatest composers)
    ISBN 0-516-04538-5
    1. Copland, Aaron, 1900-   --Juvenile literature.
    2. Composers--United States--Biography--Juvenile literature.
    [1. Copland, Aaron, 1900- . 2. Composers.] I. Title.
    II. Series: Venezia, Mike. Getting to know the world's greatest composers.
    ML3930.C66V4   1995
    780' .92--dc20
    [B]   94-36344
                               CIP
                               AC MN

Aaron Copland in 1956

Aaron Copland was one of America's greatest composers. He was born in 1900, right at the beginning of a new century and the age of modern times. Aaron not only loved to write music—he also loved teaching people how to enjoy it.

Aaron Copland's best-known music
sounds crisp and clear and simple. It often
gives you a feeling of being out west at
an exciting rodeo, or in wide-open spaces,
or in a peaceful countryside. Some people
have a hard time figuring out how

Aaron Copland was able to write music like this, since he spent most of his life in a big city. Aaron didn't think it was necessary to live in the places he wrote music about. With his great imagination, he could just about picture himself being there.

Aaron grew up in busy Brooklyn, New York. He had two older brothers and two older sisters. His parents owned a big department store. The whole family helped out there.

Even when he was very young, Aaron helped out by working as a salesman in the toy department.

Aaron Copland started showing an interest in music when he was about seven years old. He spent hours listening to records on his cousin's phonograph, which was a new invention at that time.

Aaron also started pestering his sister
Laurine whenever she practiced the piano.
He finally got her to give him some lessons.
Aaron started to make up his own songs right
away. When he was a teenager, he persuaded
his parents to send him to a "real" teacher.

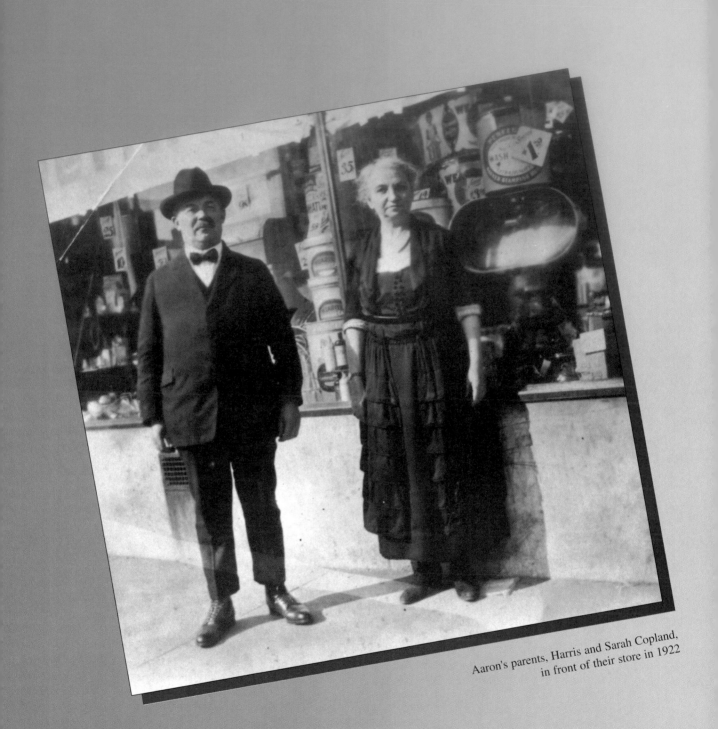

Aaron's parents, Harris and Sarah Copland,
in front of their store in 1922

Mr. and Mrs. Copland agreed to pay for Aaron's lessons as long as he found his own teacher. The Coplands thought it was important to give their children responsibility and the best opportunities they could.

Both of Aaron's parents had come to America from Russia at a time when many people in Russia were homeless and had no money. Aaron's father often reminded his children of what a great country the United States was, and how lucky they were to be there.

Aaron always remembered what his father said, especially when he began to write his most famous music.

At the beginning of the twentieth century, when Aaron Copland was growing up, people in America were just getting used to modern life. There were all kinds of modern inventions popping up.

Battle of Lights, Coney Island, Mardi Gras,
by Joseph Stella, 1913

Artists and writers were trying out modern ideas, too. It seemed like everything was becoming new and exciting—everything except America's classical music.

Abstraction on Spectrum (Organization, 5), by Stanton MacDonald Wright, ca. 1914-17

Classical-music lovers in America seemed satisfied listening to music that had been written years before by great European composers like Mozart, Beethoven, and Chopin.

So, Beethoven, Chopin, what's new?

Austrian composer Wolfgang Amadeus Mozart (1756-1791)

German composer Ludwig van Beethoven (1770-1827)

Polish composer Frédéric Chopin (1810-1849)

Aaron learned about and respected these composers, but he felt it was important to learn about American music and modern composers, too.

Nadia Boulanger

When Aaron was twenty years old, he got a chance to study music in Paris, France. Paris was the modern-music center of the world. Aaron's teacher was Nadia Boulanger, one of the best composition teachers of the twentieth century.

Watercolor sketch of a set design for Maurice Ravel's ballet *Daphnis and Chloe,* by Leon Bakst, 1912

Many of her students went on to become famous composers. Aaron was very excited. He started learning about modern composers, like Igor Stravinsky and Maurice Ravel. These composers weren't afraid to try new and different things. They often shocked people with musical sounds that had never been heard before.

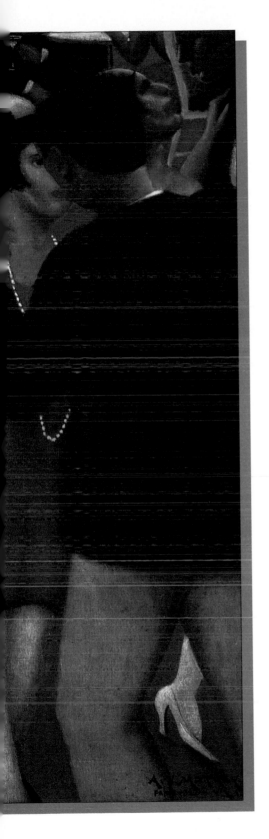

While he was studying in Paris, Aaron sometimes took time off and traveled with his friends to different countries. On one trip, Aaron noticed that wherever he went, musicians were playing a lively kind of music called jazz. Even though jazz had been invented in America, it was becoming very popular in Europe. Since Aaron was interested in writing American-sounding music, he thought it might be a good idea to add some jazz sounds to the modern classical music he was starting to write.

Blues, by American artist
Archibald John Motley, Jr., 1929

The music Aaron came up with was very original. Nadia Boulanger liked it a lot and asked Aaron to play it for some of her important friends. One of those friends was Serge Koussevitzky, the new music conductor of the Boston Symphony Orchestra. Mr. Koussevitzky liked Aaron's music, too, and agreed to play one of his new pieces at a concert.

When Aaron's *Symphony for Organ and Orchestra* was played, a lot of people didn't like it. Some of them even booed!

They probably didn't care for the modern sound, especially the jazzy parts. At the time, Aaron Copland didn't really mind if people disliked his music. He knew it might take a while for people to get used to it, because it sounded so different from music they had heard before.

Aaron kept adding jazz rhythms, and experimented with other sounds to make his music as original and modern as possible. For a while, his music became more and more complicated. Sometimes, even musicians in the orchestra found it almost too hard to play. Aaron started to notice that only people who were very serious about music were able to understand and appreciate his new music. This wasn't what he wanted at all. Aaron Copland wanted everyone in America to be able to enjoy his music.

Baile en Tehuantepec,
by Mexican artist Diego Rivera, ca. 1935

Right around this time, Aaron got
a chance to visit Mexico. He noticed
that music was much more a part of
people's lives in Mexico than it was
in the United States.

Aaron heard people playing guitars and singing, and saw people dancing wherever he went. Once, when he went to a large dance hall, Aaron became so excited by the joyful, fast-moving music being played that he decided to write a music piece about Mexico. Aaron took bits and pieces of Mexican folk tunes, and put them together with his own music. Aaron called his new piece *El Salón México*. When you listen to it, it's easy to imagine the people and beautiful countryside of Mexico.

hen *El Salón México* was played, it gave people a happy feeling. The piece soon became very popular. Aaron realized that he was on the right track to writing music that more people could enjoy.

In 1938, Aaron was asked to write some music for a ballet about the legendary Wild West outlaw Billy the Kid.

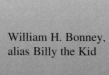

William H. Bonney, alias Billy the Kid

A scene from Aaron Copland's ballet *Billy the Kid* as performed by the Dance Theatre of Harlem

Aaron had always loved stories about the Old West. He thought he would write *Billy the Kid* in the same way that he wrote *El Salón México*. But instead of using parts of Mexican folk songs, Aaron used American folk songs in his piece.

In *Billy the Kid*, you can hear familiar folk songs here and there, like "Git Along Little Dogies" and "Bury Me Not on the Lone Prairie." People liked hearing parts of songs they had known while they were growing up. At that time, people in America were worried. There was something going on called the Great Depression, which caused many Americans to lose their jobs and savings and become poor. It also looked like America was about to get into a serious war that had already started in Europe.

Cradling Wheat,
by Thomas Hart Benton, 1938

Artists, writers, and composers began
looking around at the everyday things
that made America great. They put what
they saw and heard into paintings, books,
and music. Their works gave people a
feeling of comfort and hope, and helped
make them proud of their country.

Aaron Copland went on to compose many famous pieces, including *Fanfare for the Common Man* (part of his *Third Symphony*) and the ballets *Rodeo* and *Appalachian Spring*. Even though he used parts of American hymns and American cowboy, riverboat, and railroad songs, Aaron combined them with his own music to come up with a very special, exciting, and beautiful all-American sound.

A scene from *Appalachian Spring*, as performed by the Martha Graham Dance Company

Aaron also went to Hollywood for a while and wrote some music for movies. He even won an Academy Award for the music he wrote for a movie called *The Heiress.*

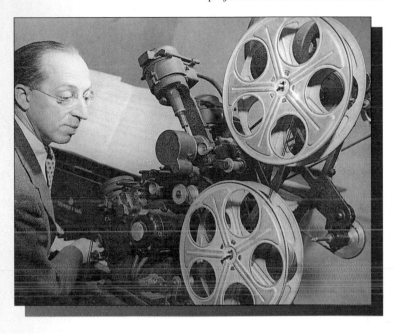

Aaron Copland composing music for a film while watching the film on a miniature projection screen called a Movieola

Aaron Copland lived to be ninety years old. As he grew older, he spent less time writing and more time conducting music and teaching. Aaron Copland told his students to always be original, to experiment with their music, and to make music that was part of modern times.

Aaron Copland conducting a rehearsal of the Boston Symphony Orchestra in 1980

Aaron Copland with one of his students

Although Aaron Copland was very busy throughout his life, he always found time to help out young composers. He worked hard to put on concerts so that many people could learn to enjoy music. He also wrote music that was just for high-school students to play in their bands and orchestras.

Today, Aaron Copland's music is as popular as ever, so it's easy to find it on the radio. There are many recordings of his music, too. You can probably check out tapes and compact discs of Aaron Copland's music from your library.